Christmas Maths

Content of the worksheets

The first section of this book (Worksheets 1-22) contains activities that are targeted towards Year 1, while the later pages (Worksheets 23-45) are targeted towards Year 2. However, you can use any of the sheets with your own class, regardless of which year groups you have. The aim should be for pupils to be engaged in enjoyable activities that provide practice of mathematical skills and knowledge at an appropriate level for them.

Year 1

Worksheet		Objective
1	Christmas tree tens	Describe and extend number sequences; count on in steps of 10.
2	Presents and crackers	Describe and extend number sequences; count on in steps of 10.
3	Christmas counting	Read and write numbers in figures.
4	Counting snowflakes	Count reliably a set of objects; read and write numbers in figures.
5	Shape decorations	Count reliably a set of objects.
6	Pattern strings	Recognise simple patterns; talk about and make repeated patterns.
7	Fill the sleigh	Count reliably at least 20 objects; begin to know addition facts for pairs of numbers up to at least 10.
8	Buying sweets with 10p	Begin to recognise that more than two numbers can be added; find totals (and change from) up to 20p.
9	Snowman shapes	Use everyday language to describe familiar 2D shapes.
10	Square puzzle	Begin to know subtraction facts for all pairs of numbers up to 10.
11	Buying biscuits with 20p	Begin to recognise that more than two numbers can be added; find totals (and change) from up to 20p.
12	Sorting trees	Use vocabulary related to length; compare two lengths – extend to more than two.
13	Paper patterns	Use one or more shape to make, describe and continue repeating patterns.
14	Christmas addition (1)	Begin to know addition facts for all pairs of numbers to at least 10.
15	Christmas addition (2)	Begin to know addition facts for all pairs of numbers to at least 10.
16	Wrap it up!	Solve simple word problems in 'real life' contexts; add or subtract a pair of numbers.
17	Christmas stockings	Solving problems – reasoning about shapes.
18	Delivering presents	Count on in twos.
19	Away in a manger	Learn doubles of all numbers to at least 5.
20	Make it match! (1)	Learn doubles of numbers to 9
21	Make it match! (2)	Learn doubles of numbers to 9.
22	Christmas time	Understand and use the vocabulary related to time; read the time from clocks.

Year 2

Worksheet		Objective
23	Number words	Read and write numbers in figures and words.
24	How many puddings?	Read and write numbers in figures and words.
25	How many crackers?	Read and write numbers in figures and words.
26	Guess how many	Understand and use the vocabulary of estimation; give a sensible estimate for a number of objects.
27	Up in the sky!	Understand and use the vocabulary of estimation; give a sensible estimate for a number of objects.
28	Finding half	Begin to recognise and find one half and one quarter of shapes and of small numbers of objects.
29	Finding quarters	Begin to recognise and find one half and one quarter of shapes and of small numbers of objects. Begin to recognise that two halves or four quarters make one whole and that two quarters and one half are equivalent.
30	Halves and quarters	Begin to recognise and find one half and one quarter of shapes and of small numbers of objects.
31	Christmas present puzzle	To solve a mathematical puzzle recognising simple patterns and relationships and explaining how the problem was solved.
32	Buying decorations with 50p	Solve problems including money; finding totals.
33	Change from 50p	Solve problems including money; finding totals and giving change.
34	Change from £5	Solve problems including money; finding totals and giving change.
35	Bells in squares	Describe and extend number sequences.
36	Two each	Know multiplication facts for the 2 times table.
37	Light up the house	Know multiplication facts for the 2 times table.
38	Light up the sleigh	Know multiplication facts for the 10 times table.
39	Light up the tree	Begin to know multiplication facts for the 5 times table.
40	Christmas timetable	Read the time to the nearest hour and half hour.
41	Measuring up	Measuring lines to the nearest centimetre.
42	Santa's sleigh	Measuring lines to the nearest centimetre.
43	All year round	Know in order the months of the year.
44	Christmas countdown	Know significant times in the year.
45	Chrismas Su Doku	Solve mathematical puzzles

Christmas tree tens

Name:  Date:

Draw a Christmas tree 🎄 in square number 4.
Count on ten and draw another Christmas tree.
Keep counting on in tens and drawing a tree
each time. Colour your trees green.

1	2	3	4	5	6	7	8	9	10
11	12	13	14	15	16	17	18	19	20
21	22	23	24	25	26	27	28	29	30
31	32	33	34	35	36	37	38	39	40
41	42	43	44	45	46	47	48	49	50
51	52	53	54	55	56	57	58	59	60
61	62	63	64	65	66	67	68	69	70
71	72	73	74	75	76	77	78	79	80
81	82	83	84	85	86	87	88	89	90
91	92	93	94	95	96	97	98	99	100

Which numbers have Christmas trees?

☐ ☐ ☐ ☐ ☐ ☐ ☐ ☐ ☐ ☐

Notes for teachers
Objective: Describe and extend number sequences; count on in steps of 10.
This activity helps pupils to appreciate the effect of adding ten to any number. What is obvious to adults may not necessarily be obvious to children and they may need to be shown that all the answers have a four as the units digit. Extend the activity by asking questions such as 'what is four add ten?', 'what is twenty-four add ten?', etc.

Presents and crackers

Name:    **Date:**

Draw a present 🎁 in square number 2.
Count on ten and draw another present.
Keep counting on in tens and drawing a present each time. Colour your presents red.

1	2	3	4	5	6	7	8	9	10
11	12	13	14	15	16	17	18	19	20
21	22	23	24	25	26	27	28	29	30
31	32	33	34	35	36	37	38	39	40
41	42	43	44	45	46	47	48	49	50
51	52	53	54	55	56	57	58	59	60
61	62	63	64	65	66	67	68	69	70
71	72	73	74	75	76	77	78	79	80
81	82	83	84	85	86	87	88	89	90
91	92	93	94	95	96	97	98	99	100

Now draw a cracker 🎉 in square number 7.
Count on ten and draw another cracker.
Keep counting on in tens and drawing another cracker each time. Colour your crackers yellow.

Notes for teachers
Objective: Describe and extend number sequences; count on in steps of 10.
This activity follows on from Worksheet 1 in helping pupils to appreciate the effect of adding ten to any number. Extend the activity by asking questions such as 'what is seven add ten?', 'what is twenty-two add ten?', etc.

Worksheet 3: Christmas counting

Name: Date:

1 2 3 4 5 6 7 8 9

Count the objects in each box and write the correct number.

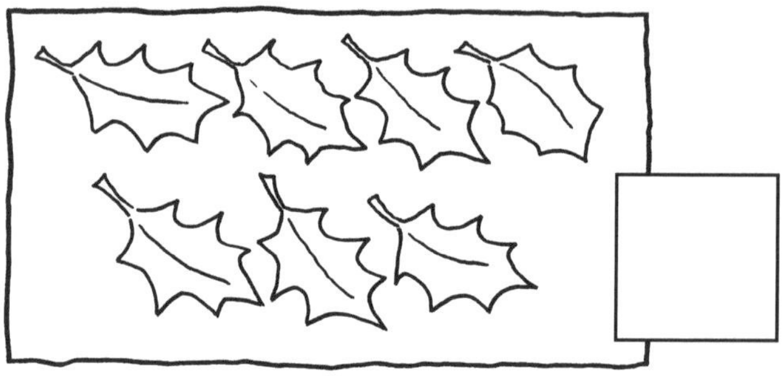

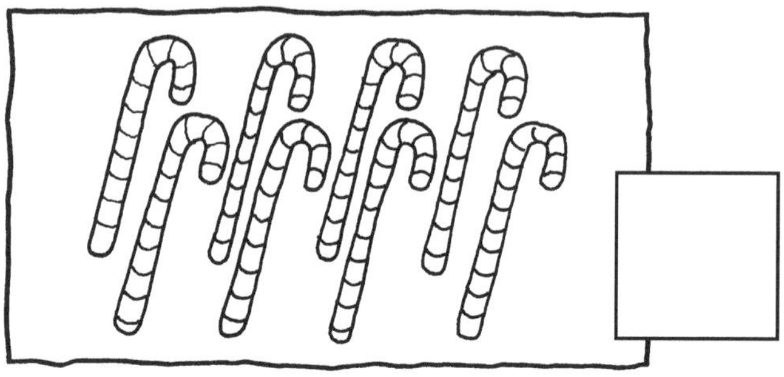

Notes for teachers
Objective: Read and write numbers in figures
This is both a counting and writing activity. Support the children in writing the numerals correctly. Observing every pupil to see how they write their numbers can reveal unexpected difficulties.

Andrew Brodie: Christmas Maths 5–7 © A & C Black Publishers Ltd. 2006

Counting snowflakes

Name:  **Date:**

Count the snowflakes that you can see through each window. Write the numbers.

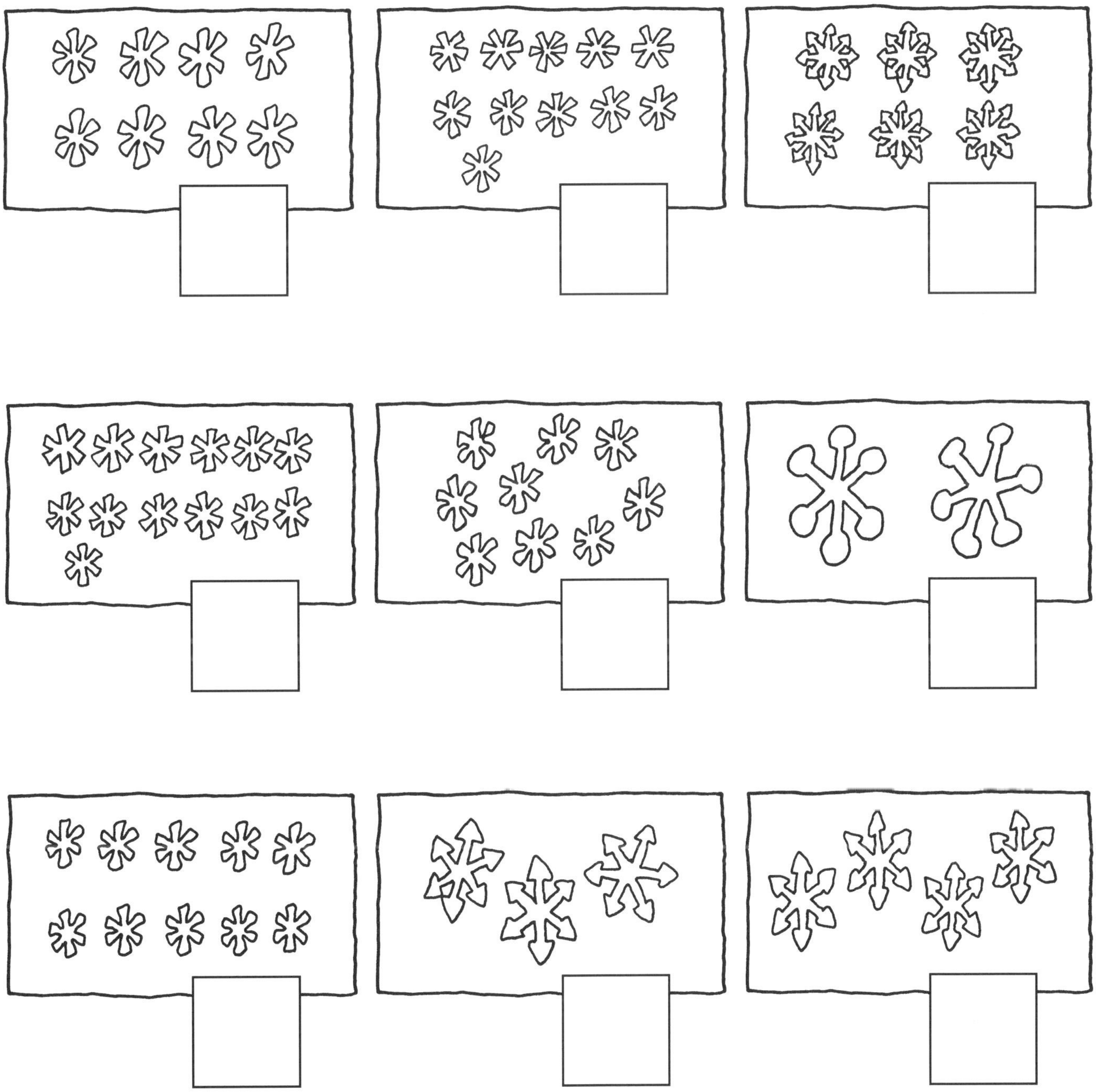

Notes for teachers
Objective: Count reliably a set of objects; read and write numbers in figures.
Pupils may need to be shown strategies for counting, particularly with larger numbers, e.g. they could cross out each snowflake as they count it. However, it is more effective to work systematically, by starting at one side of a picture and working across.

Shape decorations

Name:    Date:

Count the shapes and write the correct numbers in each box. Colour the shapes.

☐ Colour the circles red.
circles

☐ Colour the stars yellow.
stars

☐ Colour the squares green.
squares

☐ Colour the triangles blue.
triangles

☐ Colour the angel yellow.
angel

Notes for teachers
Objective: Count reliably a set of objects
As with the previous worksheet, pupils may need strategies for counting the objects to avoid getting confused by counting the wrong pictures or by counting the same picture twice.

Pattern strings

Name:  Date:

Continue the pattern along each string.

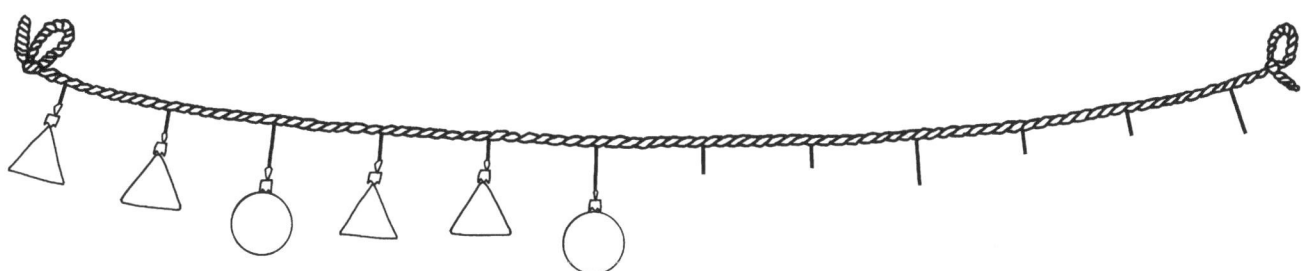

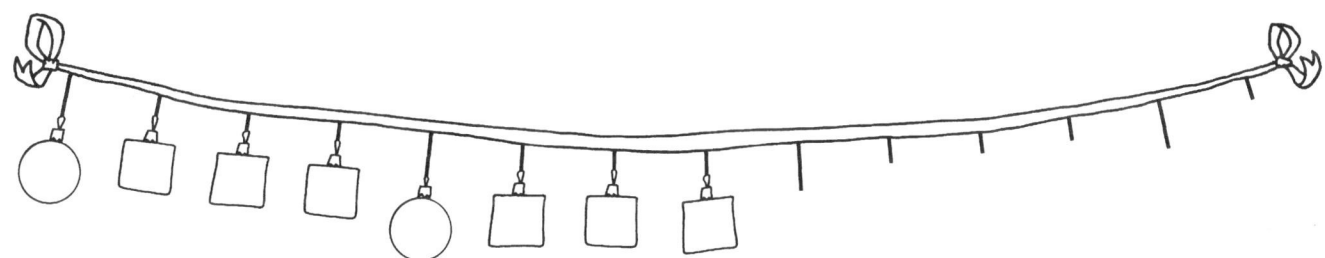

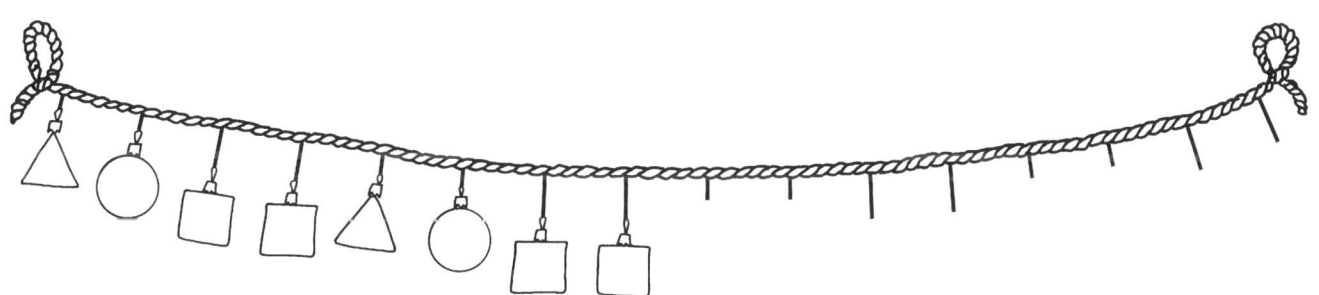

Now colour the decorations.

Notes for teachers
Objective: Recognise simple patterns; talk about and make repeated patterns.
A surprisingly difficult task, the pupils will need support in recognising the pattern on each line and then continuing it in the correct sequence.

Worksheet 7: Fill the sleigh

Name:

Date:

You will need: 2 dice marked 1 to 6; coloured pencils
Ask your teacher how to play the game.

Name:

Name:

Notes for teachers
Objective: Count reliably at least 20 objects; begin to know addition facts for all pairs of numbers up to at least 10.
Whilst most of the children may use dice with spots on, you could differentiate this activity by giving higher attainers dice with numbers on.
How to Play
Each player chooses a sleigh. Players take it in turns to roll both dice. One gift present is coloured—the present number must be either the number rolled on one of the dice or the total of the two dice added together. If the scores rolled are already coloured, the player misses that turn. The winner is the first to have all their presents coloured.

Buying sweets with 10p

Name: Date:

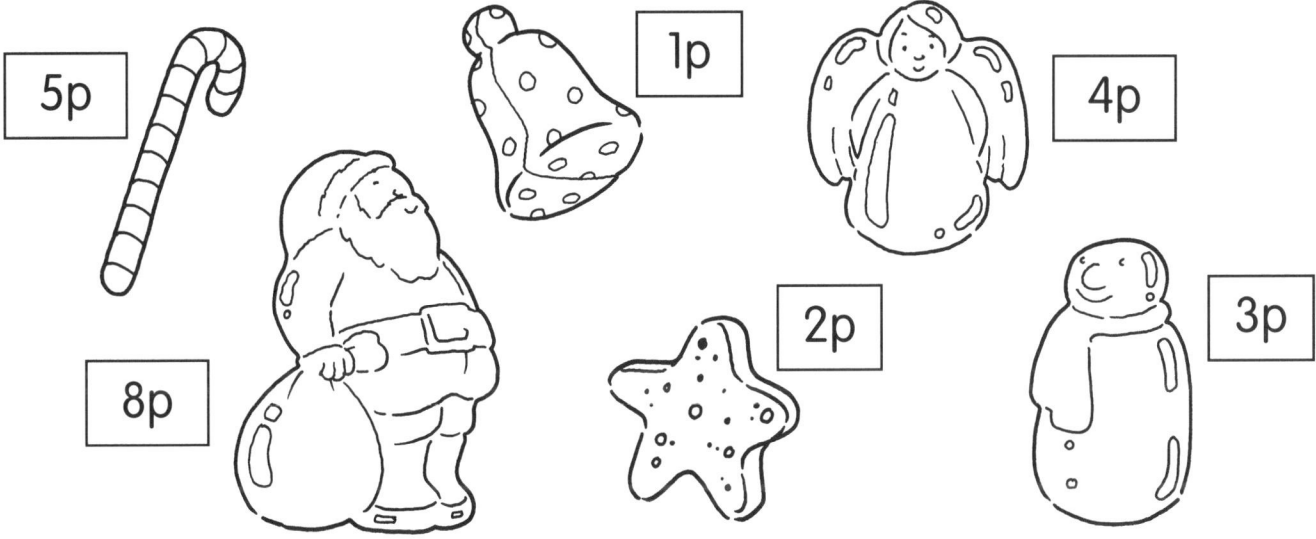

Find different ways to spend 10p on sweets.
Show your answers in the spaces below. You can use pictures or numbers.

Notes for teachers
Objective: Begin to recognise that more than two numbers can be added; find totals (and change) from up to 20p.
This activity can be completed pictorially by the children or presented as 'money sums'. Provide extra paper for children to use for showing more 'money sums'. An extension could be to ask pupils to add the cost of two items and calculate the change from 10p. You could also ask pupils to add together any three items–some of these would extend pupils beyond 10p.

Andrew Brodie: Christmas Maths 5–7 © A & C Black Publishers Ltd. 2006

Snowman shapes

Name:  Date:

Look carefully at the picture below.
Colour the triangles green.
Colour the circles red.
Colour the rectangles blue.
Colour the squares yellow.
Colour the hexagons purple.

Fill in the missing numbers.

I found ☐ triangles

I found ☐ circles

I found ☐ rectangles

I found ☐ squares

I found ☐ hexagons

Notes for teachers
Objective: Use everyday language to describe familiar 2D shapes
Talk to children about the properties of the shapes they have identified as part of this task.

Square puzzle

Name:  Date:

Do the subtraction in each square.
If the answer is 4 colour the square green.
If the answer is 7 colour the square blue.
Colour the star yellow.
Colour all the other squares orange.

10-1	5-4	5-3	☆	7-5	10-8	7-6
7-7	5-3	6-3	10-6	8-7	9-6	8-5
9-0	0-0	9-5	8-4	7-3	10-4	8-7
7-6	7-3	6-2	4-0	8-4	10-6	8-2
1-0	1-1	10-4	8-1	5-4	8-8	9-8
10-2	9-1	9-2	10-3	7-0	8-0	7-1
4-3	3-2	8-1	9-2	10-3	5-5	2-2

What picture did you find?   I found a _____

Notes for teachers
Objective: Begin to know subtraction facts for all pairs of numbers up to 10
Correctly completed, the picture should show a Christmas tree in a rectangular pot.

Buying biscuits with 20p

Name: Date:

Find different ways to spend 20p on biscuits.
Show your ways to spend the money in the spaces below.
You can use pictures or numbers.

Notes for teachers
Objective: Recognise that more than two numbers can be added; find totals (and change from) up to 20p.
This activity can be completed pictorially by the children or presented as 'money sums'. An extension for the more able could be to investigate ways to buy any two biscuits and calculate the change from 20p. Provide extra paper for children to use for showing more 'money sums'.

Worksheet 12

Sorting trees

Name:

 Date:

Cut out the trees. Stick them on the spaces below. Begin with the **tallest** and end with the **shortest**.

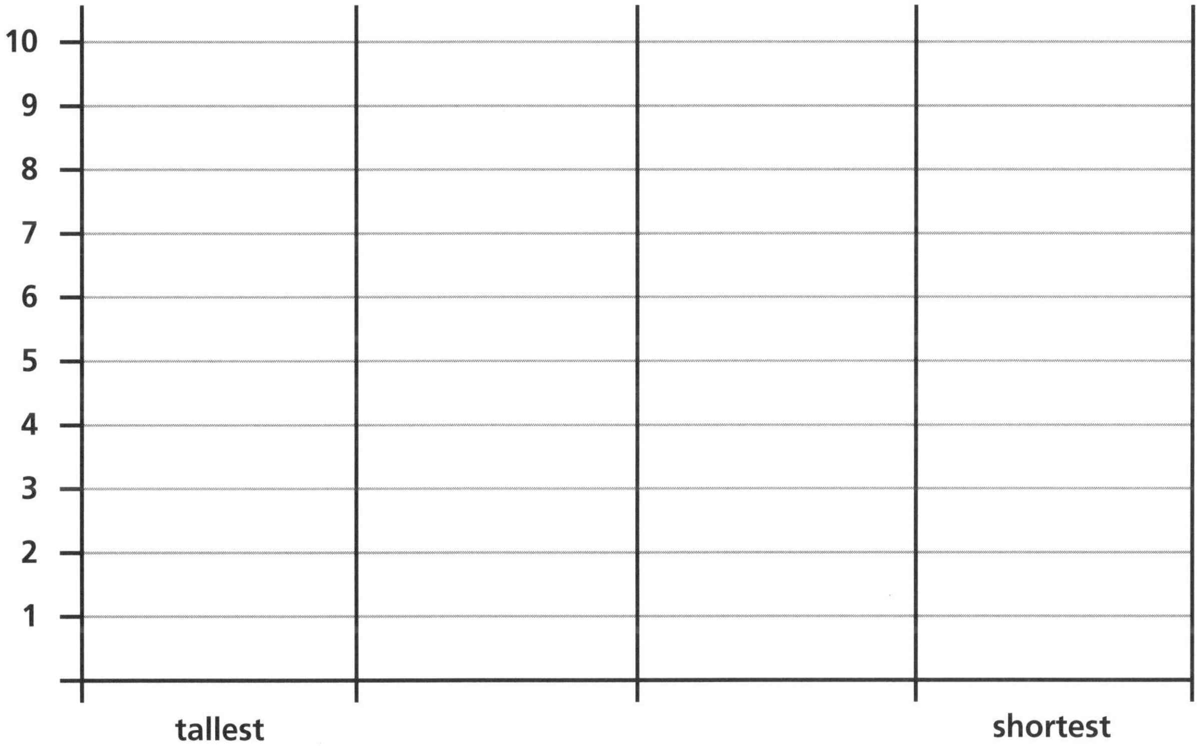

tallest   shortest

Notes for teachers
Objective: Use vocabulary related to length; compare two lengths – extend to more than two.
Ensure pupils have all four trees correctly placed on the chart before they are stuck down. Talk to the pupils using the terms taller, tallest, shorter, shortest. Help the child work out the order in which the trees should be stuck on the chart.

Paper patterns

Name:

Date:

Look at the wrapping paper.
Can you finish the pattern on it?

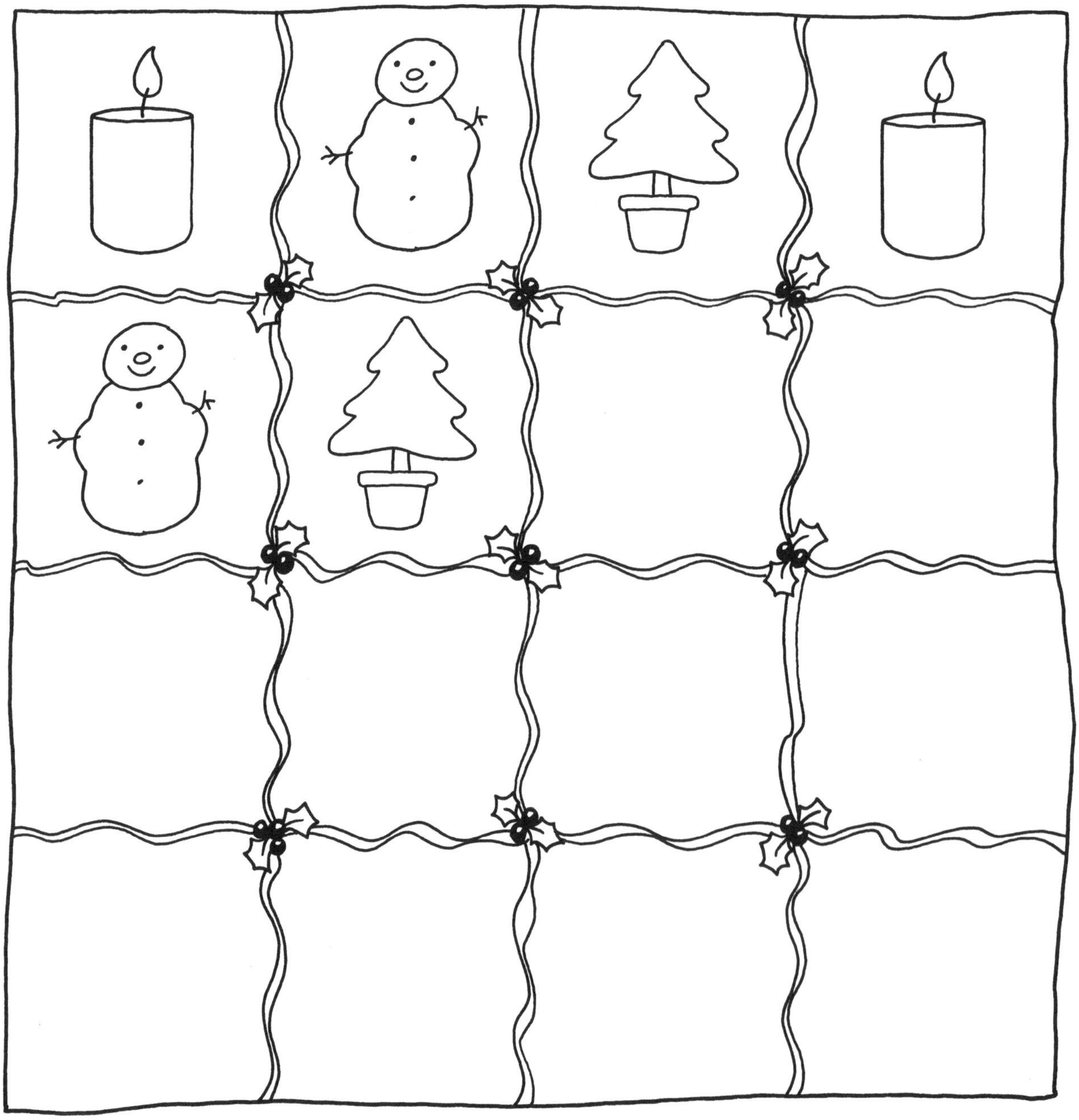

Now colour the pattern you have made.

Notes for teachers
Objective: Use one or more shape to make, describe and continue repeating patterns
Encourage pupils to colour in such a way as to consolidate the pattern.

Christmas addition (1)

Name: Date:

Cut out the squares on this worksheet.
Do each addition to find out where to stick the squares on the grid on Worksheet 15.

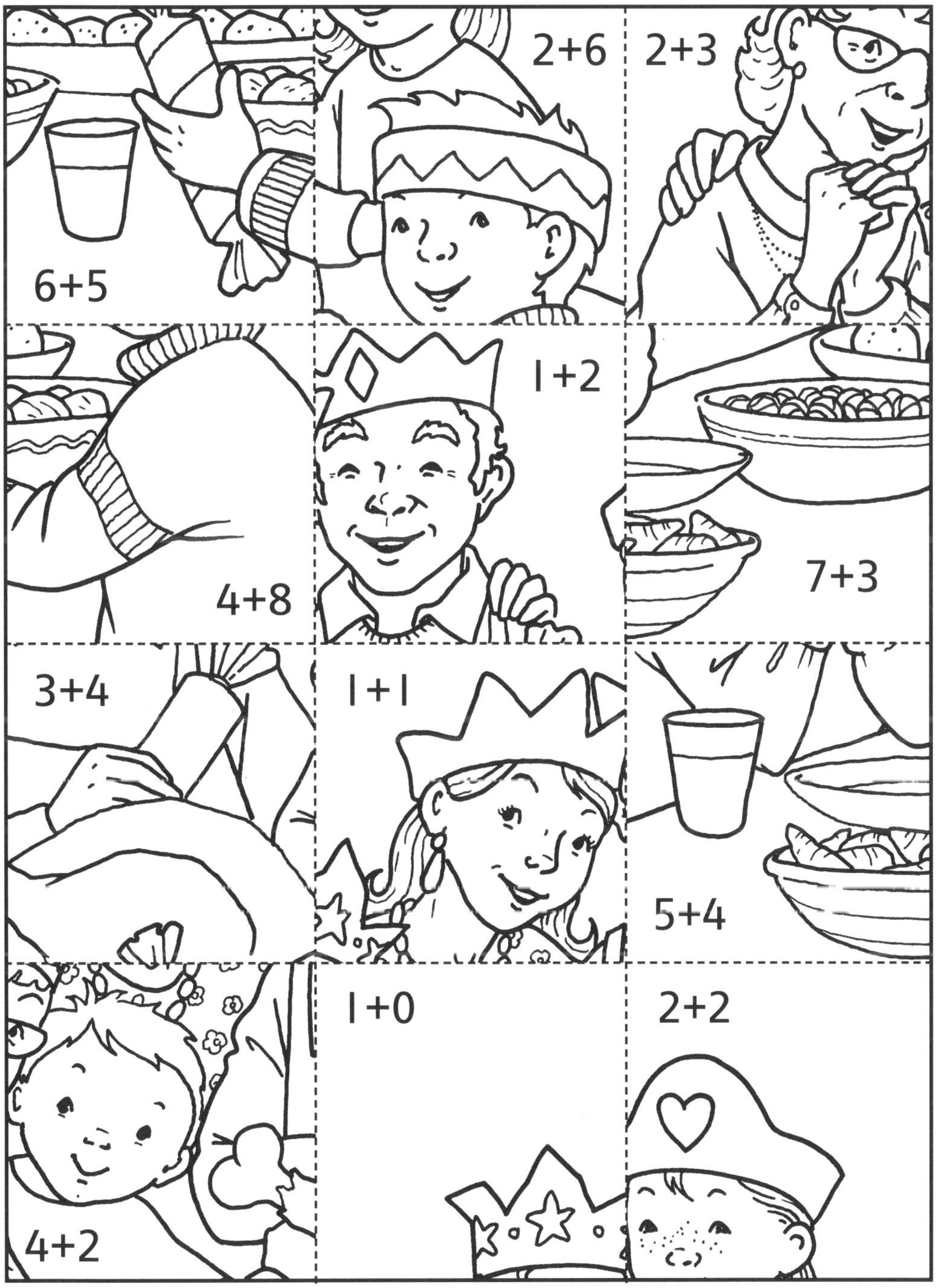

6+5	2+6	2+3
4+8	1+2	7+3
3+4	1+1	5+4
4+2	1+0	2+2

Notes for teachers
Objective: Begin to know addition facts for all pairs of numbers to at least 10
An extension/alternative is to use a festive picture or card to cut up and put calculations on according to each pupil's mathematical needs.

Christmas addition (2)

Name: Date:

Stick your squares in the correct places and colour in the picture.

1	2	3	4
5	6	7	8
9	10	11	12

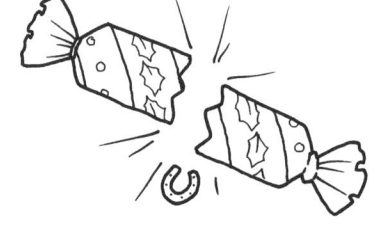
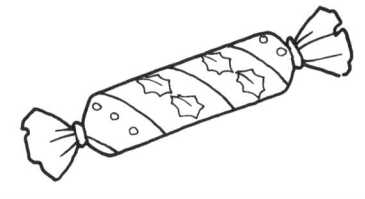

Notes for teachers
Objective: Begin to know addition facts for all pairs of numbers to at least 10
Ensure that the children have all twelve of their squares correctly placed before sticking them down. If tackled in this way the activity is self-corrective. If all the squares are stuck in the correct places they should form a picture of a very cheerful Christmas day meal.

How many puddings?

Name:  Date:

eleven   twelve   thirteen   fourteen   fifteen
sixteen   seventeen   eighteen   nineteen   twenty

Count the Christmas puddings.
Write the correct number word for each set.

→ ....

→ ....

→ ....

→ ....

→ ....

→ ....

→ ....

→ ....

Notes for teachers
Objective: Read and write numbers in figures and words
Pupils may need to be reminded of strategies for counting, particularly with the larger numbers. They are likely to need help with spelling these number words. Ask pupils which two numbers of objects are missing (thirteen and sixteen) and to draw pictures for these on the back of the sheet.

Andrew Brodie: Christmas Maths 5–7 © A & C Black Publishers Ltd. 2006

Worksheet 23: Number words

Name:  Date:

one   two   three   four   five   six
seven   eight   nine   ten

Write the correct number word for each set.

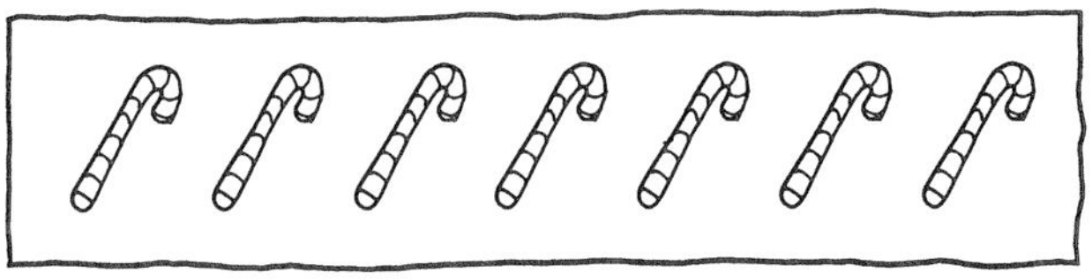

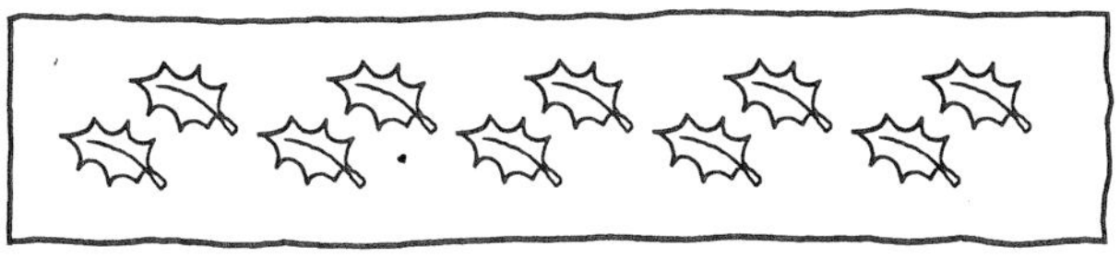

Wrap it up!

Name:  Date:

1. Dad has wrapped two presents and Mum has wrapped four presents. How many have they wrapped altogether?

    2 + 4 = ☐

2. Kitty has wrapped five presents and Harry has wrapped three presents. How many have they wrapped altogether?

    5 + 3 = ☐

3. Mum has wrapped four presents. She gives two away. How many does she have left?

    4 - 2 = ☐

    How many presents can you count altogether in the picture? ☐

Notes for teachers
Objective: Solve simple word problems in 'real' life contexts; add or subtract a pair of numbers
Some children will need help reading the questions. You could extend this work by asking pupils to draw their own pictures of parcels, then to make up mathematical questions to ask each other.

Christmas stockings

Name:

Date:

Can you make each stocking look different by using 3 different colours? You must use one colour for each stripe. You must use all 3 colours on each stocking.

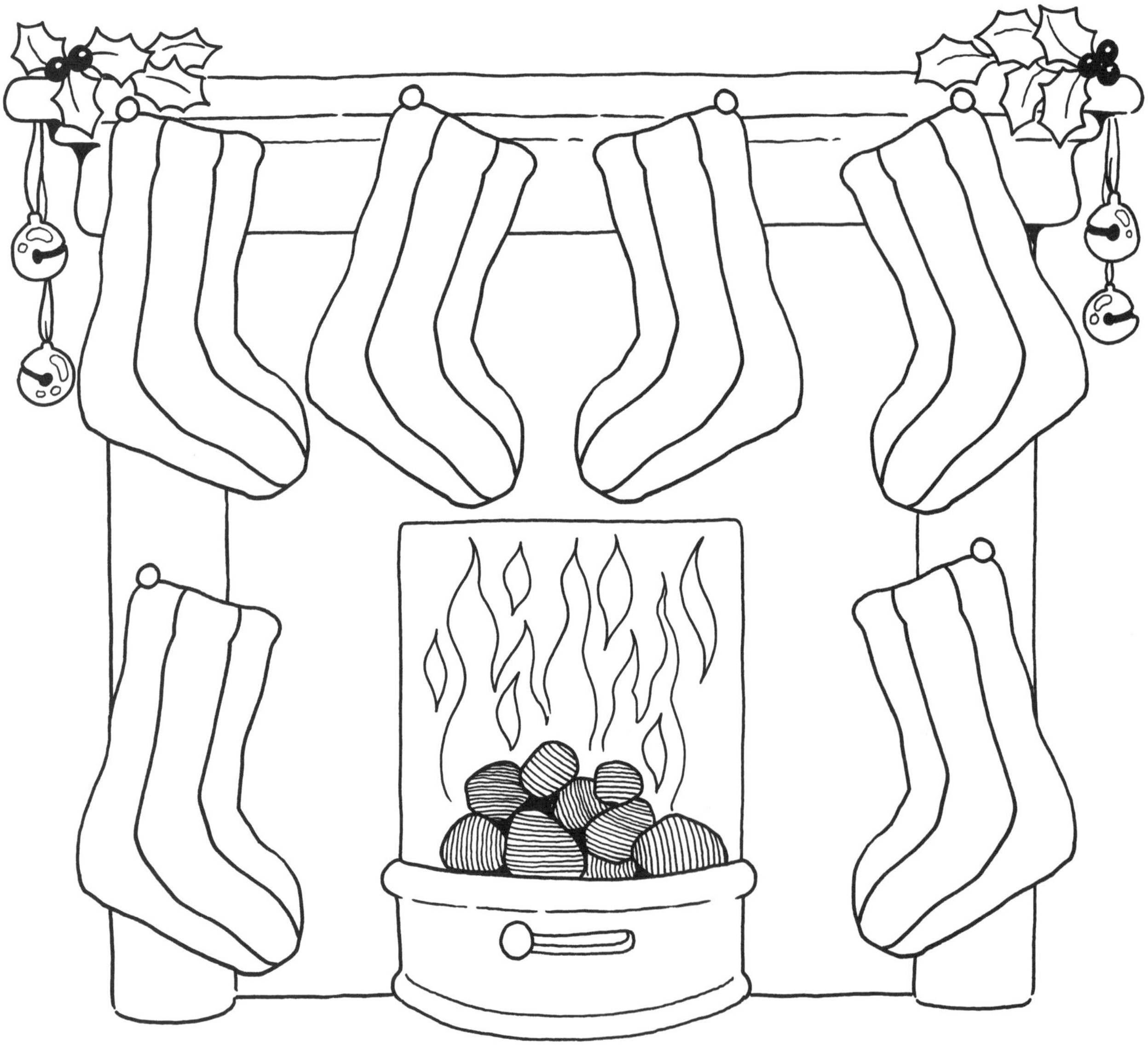

Now tell a friend how you did it.

Notes for teachers
Objective: Solve problems – reasoning about shapes
Ensure that pupils select three contrasting colours before they begin. An extension could be to ask pupils how many more stockings could be coloured if they could repeat a colour on the same stocking, eg all three stripes the same colour, or two stripes of one colour and one of another.

Delivering presents

Name:  Date:

Add 2 to the number on each present to show Santa which house to deliver it to.

Present number 5 goes to house number 7. Draw lines from each of the other presents to the correct houses.

Notes for teachers
Objective: Count on in twos
Help the children by looking at each parcel in turn, adding two to its number then drawing a line joining the parcel to the appropriate house. You could discuss with the children that the houses on one side of the street are usually odd and on the opposite side, even.

Andrew Brodie: Christmas Maths 5–7 © A & C Black Publishers Ltd. 2006

Away in a manger

Name:  **Date:**

Look at the picture.
Colour double 3 yellow.
Colour double 4 orange
Colour double 2 green.
Colour double 1 red.

Colour double 7 dark blue.
Colour double 6 brown.
Colour double 10 grey.

Notes for teachers
Objective: Learn doubles of all numbers to at least 5
You may encourage pupils to work out all the doubles and write them on the sheet by the appropriate colour before they begin to colour the picture. If there are any pupils who cannot read the colour names you could make a mark in the appropriate colour by each word.

Andrew Brodie: Christmas Maths 5–7 © A & C Black Publishers Ltd. 2006

Make it match! (1)

Name:    Date:

Cut out the squares.

Put the pairs of pictures together by using doubles.
Picture 7 matches picture 14.

Put all the pairs of squares together to make a Christmas picture. Stick the pictures on to Worksheet 21.

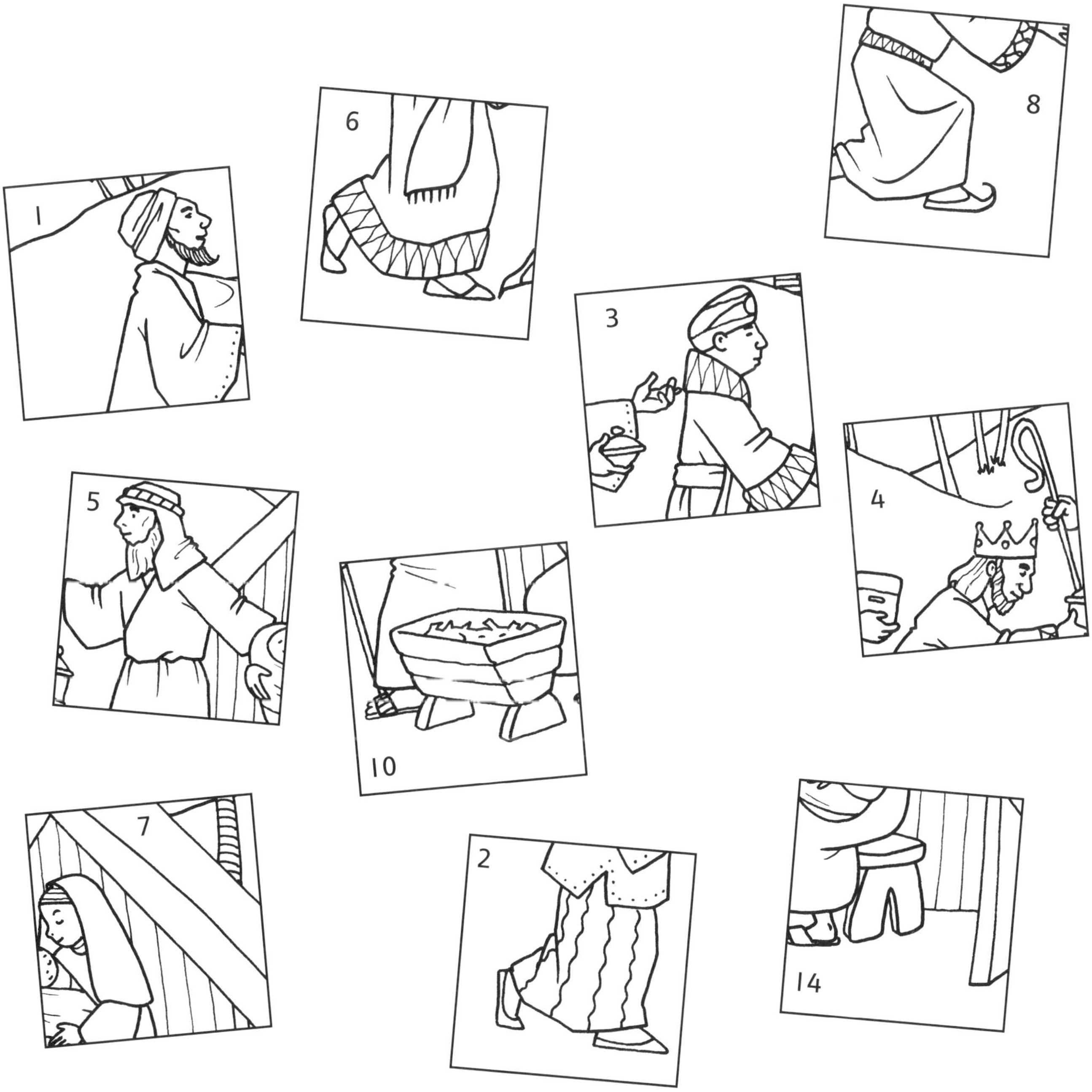

Notes for teachers
Objective: Learn doubles of numbers to 9

Make it match! (2)

Name:  Date:

Stick the pictures from Worksheet 20 on here.

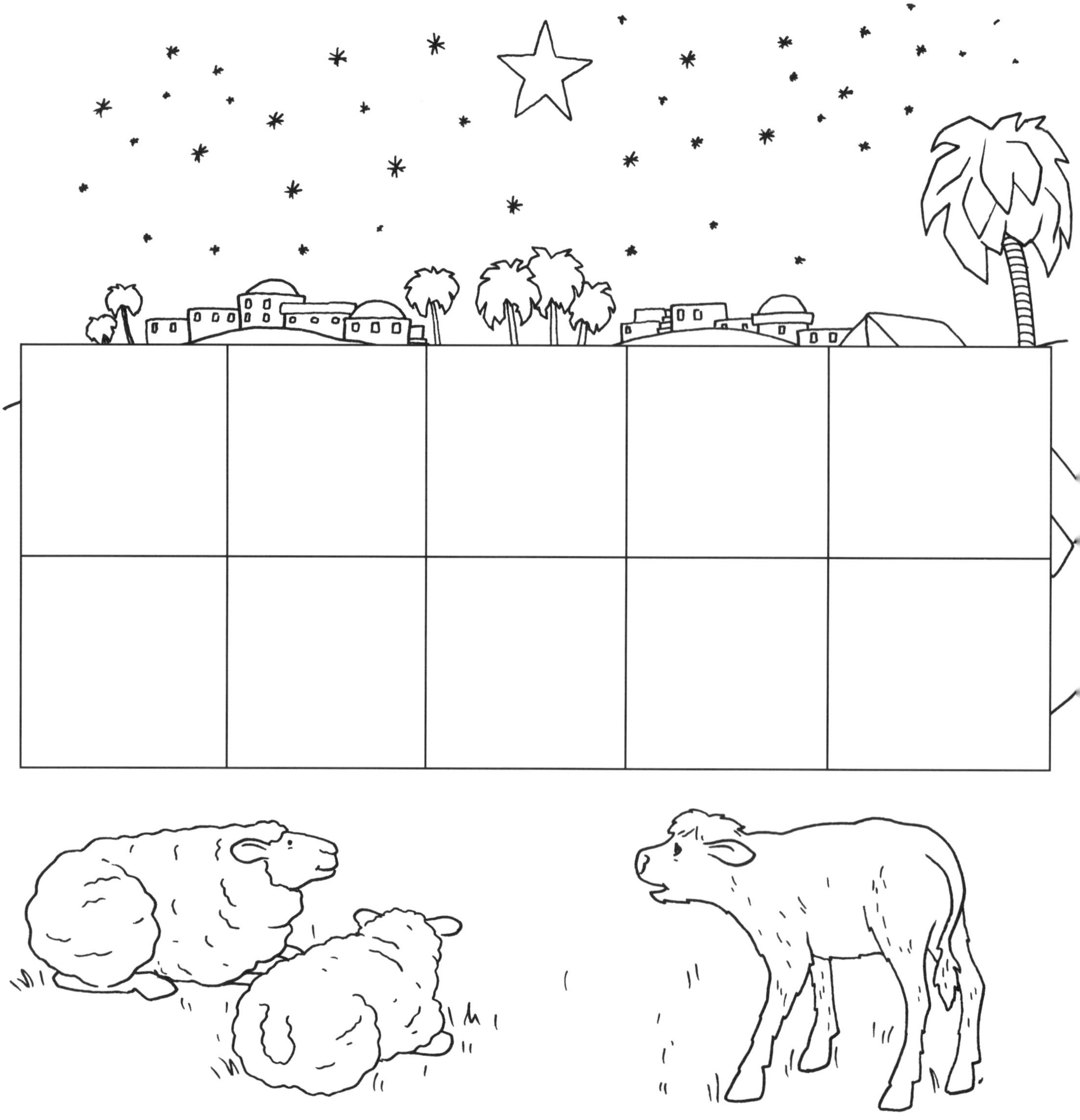

Notes for teachers
Objective: Learn doubles of numbers to 9
The pictures created from Worksheet 20 can be stuck on to the scene on this sheet. Take the opportunity to remind the child of the doubling process.

Christmas time

Name:  Date:

What will you be doing on Christmas Day?
Write five sentences about your day and fill in the time on the clock faces.

Notes for teachers
Objective: Understand and use the vocabulary related to time; read the time from clocks
Use this near the very end of term. You will need to be sensitive to the religions that are represented in your class; if you feel that some children will not be celebrating Christmas then you may decide not to use this worksheet. Encourage the children to think quietly about what happens on Christmas Day. Discuss the types of things that could happen: getting up in the morning, emptying stockings, visiting grandparents, going to church, having lunch, watching television, etc. Support them in showing appropriate times on the clocks and in writing a sentence next to each clock.

Andrew Brodie: Christmas Maths 5–7 © A & C Black Publishers Ltd. 2006

Worksheet 23: Number words

Name: Date:

| one | two | three | four | five | six |
| seven | eight | | nine | ten | |

Write the correct number word for each set.

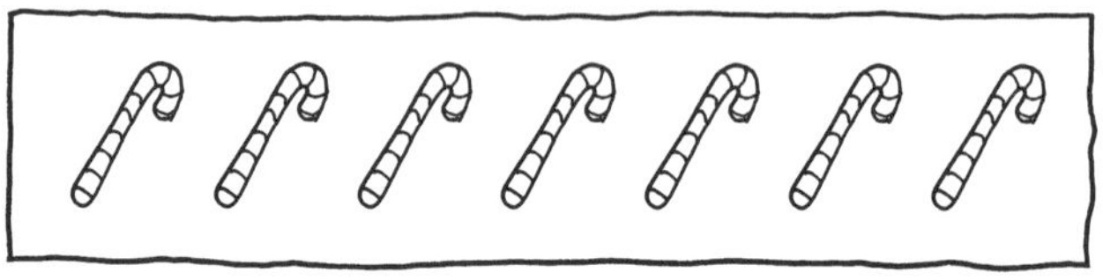

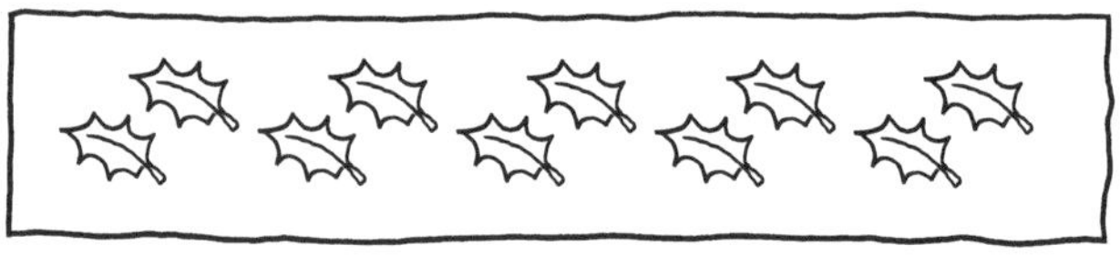

Notes for teachers
Objective: Read and write numbers in figures and words
This activity provides an opportunity to check and support both spelling and handwriting.

26   Andrew Brodie: Christmas Maths 5–7 © A & C Black Publishers Ltd. 2006

How many puddings?

Name:  Date:

eleven   twelve   thirteen   fourteen   fifteen
sixteen   seventeen   eighteen   nineteen   twenty

Count the Christmas puddings.
Write the correct number word for each set.

→ ....

→ ....

→ ....

→ ....

→ ....

→ ....

→ ....

→ ....

Notes for teachers
Objective: Read and write numbers in figures and words
Pupils may need to be reminded of strategies for counting, particularly with the larger numbers. They are likely to need help with spelling these number words. Ask pupils which two numbers of objects are missing (thirteen and sixteen) and to draw pictures for these on the back of the sheet.

How many crackers?

Name:  Date:

How many crackers can you find in the picture? ☐

Match the numbers to the words.
Copy the number words.
One has been done for you.

27	fifty-two	fifty-two
33	forty-eight	....
79	eighty-five	....
48	sixty-six	....
52	twenty-seven	....
66	seventy-nine	....
94	thirty-three	....
85	ninety-four	....

Notes for teachers
Objective: Read and write numbers in figures and words
There are thirty-two crackers on the page. Pupils are likely to need help in spelling the words. It is worthwhile pointing out that 'forty' is spelt in a different way to 'four' and 'fourteen'.

Guess how many

Name:  Date:

How many reindeer do you think there are in this picture?

I estimate the number of reindeer is ....

Now count the reindeer.

There are .... reindeer.

The difference between my estimate and the actual number is ....

Estimate: .... Elves

Actual number: ....

Difference between estimate and actual: ....

On the back of the sheet draw a large number of stars. Ask your friend to estimate how many there are. Is their estimate a good one?

Notes for teachers
Objective: Understand and use the vocabulary of estimation; give a sensible estimate for a number of objects. There are twenty-seven reindeer and seventeen elves on this page. This task provides excellent practice in the essential skill of making estimates.

Up in the sky!

Name:

 Date:

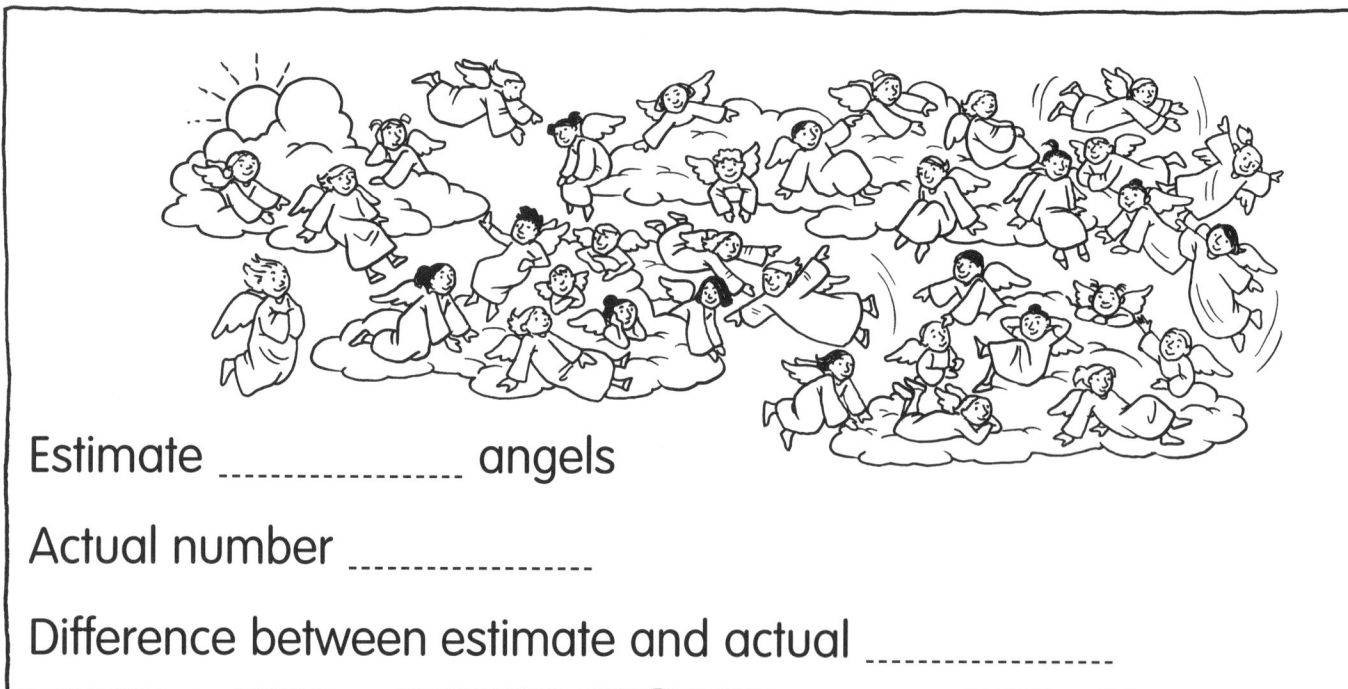

Estimate .... angels

Actual number ....

Difference between estimate and actual ....

Estimate .... stars

Actual number ....

Difference between estimate and actual ....

On the back of the sheet draw a large number of snowmen. Ask your friend to estimate how many there are. Is their estimate a good one?

Notes for teachers
Objective: Understand and use the vocabulary of estimation; give a sensible estimate for a number of objects. There are thirty-five angels and seventy-six stars on this page. This task provides further practice in making estimates. Encourage the children to think carefully before estimating. With practice their estimates should improve.

Worksheet 28: Finding half

Name:  Date:

Colour **half** of each set red and half green.

Notes for teachers
Objective: Begin to recognise and find one half and one quarter of small numbers of objects
You may wish to encourage pupils to separate each set into two equal sub sets before colouring. It is perfectly acceptable for pupils to use other colours instead of red and green, provided that one half of the items in each set is clearly one colour and the other half is another colour.

Andrew Brodie: Christmas Maths 5–7 © A & C Black Publishers Ltd. 2006

Finding quarters

Name:  Date:

Colour **one quarter** of each set of items red.
Colour **one quarter** of each set of items yellow.
Colour the rest blue.

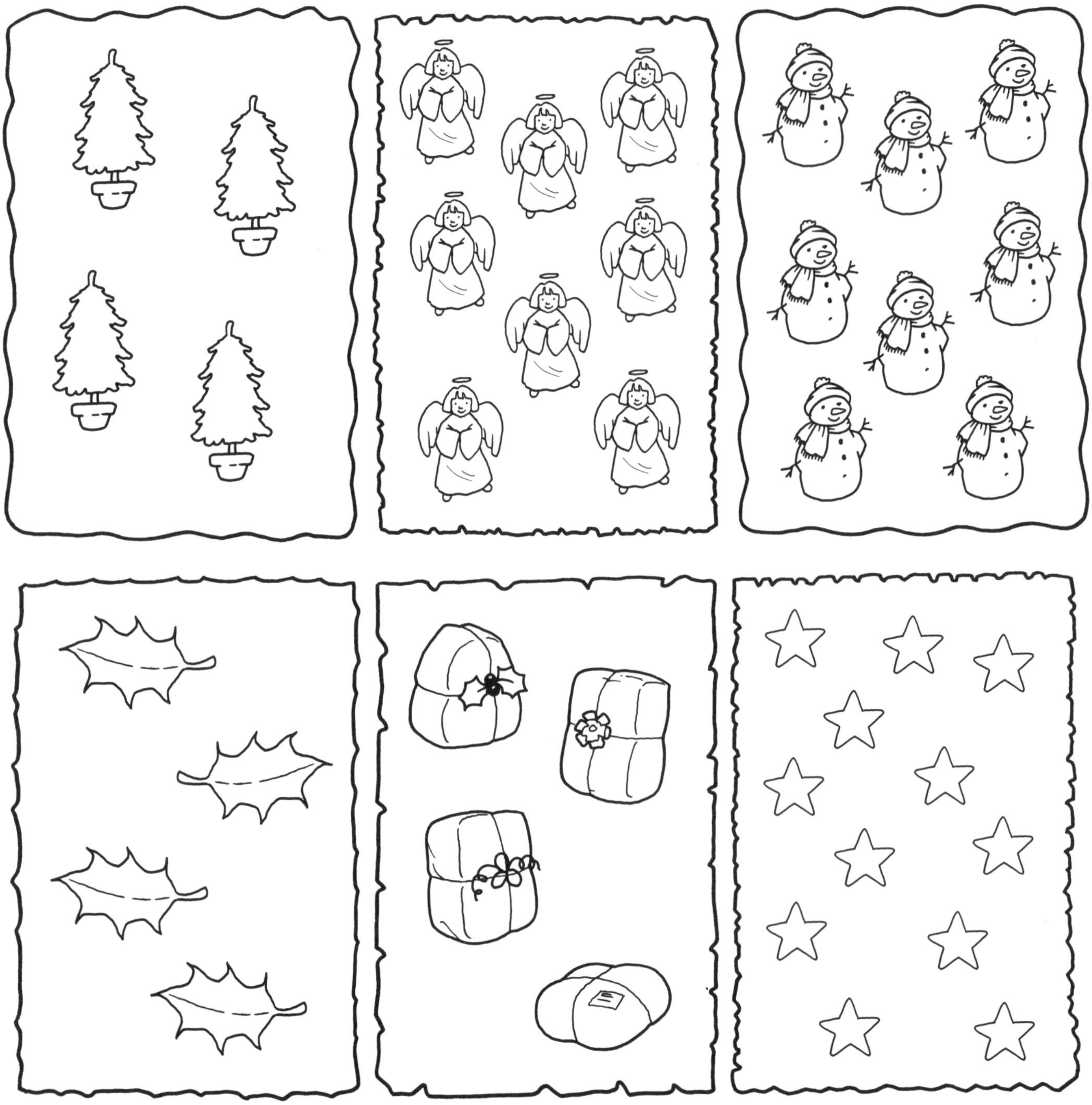

Notes for teachers
Objective: Begin to recognise and find one half and one quarter of small numbers of objects. Begin to recognise that two halves or four quarters make one whole and that two quarters and one half are equivalent.
Pupils should be encouraged to divide each set into four quarters before colouring – from this they can be helped to see that the two quarters that remain after colouring their red and yellow items is equal to one half of the set.

worksheet 30

Halves and quarters

Name: Date:

Colour **half** the tree pale green and the other **half** dark green.

Colour **half** the lights red and the other **half** yellow.

Colour **one quarter** of the tub blue, **one quarter** red, **one quarter** yellow and **one quarter** green.

Notes for teachers
Objective: Begin to recognise and find one half and one quarter of shapes and of small numbers of objects
This is a difficult task and you may decide to give the worksheet only to higher ability pupils.

Andrew Brodie: Christmas Maths 5–7 © A & C Black Publishers Ltd. 2006

Worksheet 31: Christmas present puzzle

Name: Date:

Can you give each present a different pattern of stripes? Use 4 different colours. You must use one colour for each stripe. You must use all four colours on each present.

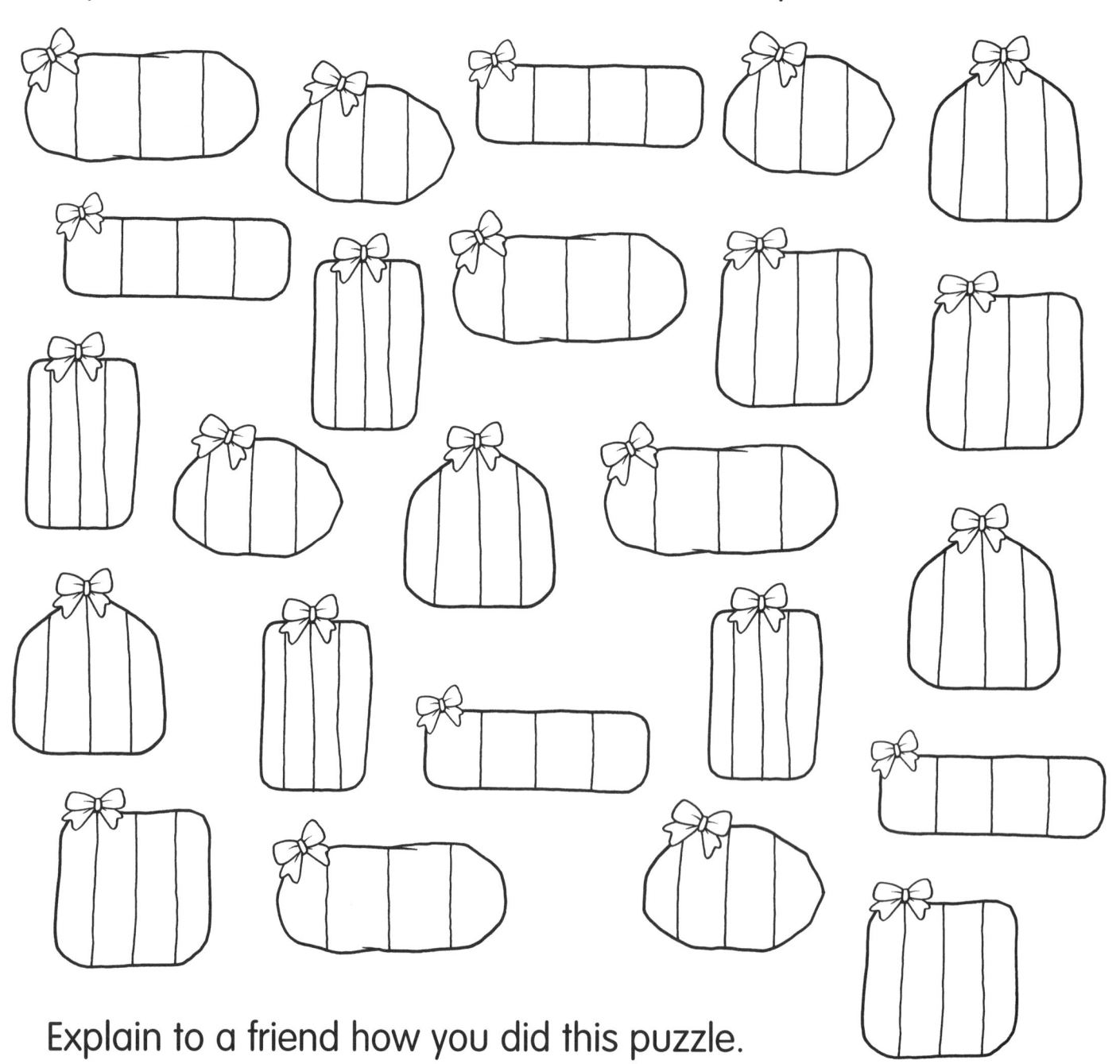

Explain to a friend how you did this puzzle.

Notes for teachers
Objective: Solve a mathematical puzzle recognising simple patterns and relationships and explaining how the problem was solved
Encourage a logical approach to this task. An extension to this activity would be to ask how many ways the presents could be coloured using just two colours or just three of the colours. Ask pupils to estimate the number they think there might be with reasons for their estimate before beginning either of the extension activities.

Andrew Brodie: Christmas Maths 5–7 © A & C Black Publishers Ltd. 2006

worksheet 32

Buying decorations with 50p

Name: Date:

Find different ways of spending 50p on tree decorations. Record your ideas in the spaces below. You may need to use the back of the sheet too.

- 20p — bauble
- 10p — bird
- 15p — star
- 5p — holly
- 6p — Santa
- 7p — angel
- 14p — snowman
- 23p — cracker

Notes for teachers
Objective: Solve problems including money; finding totals.
Pupils might need to use the back of the sheets for working out. The recording of this work might be in the form of money sums or pictorial – or of course a mixture of both. Remind pupils to use a 'p' to indicate that their answers are a number of pence.

Worksheet 33: Change from 50p

Name: Date:

If you buy the decorations shown, how much change will you get from 50p?
The first one has been done for you.

Prices: 20p (bauble), 10p (bird), 15p (star), 5p (holly), 6p (santa), 7p (angel), 14p (snowman), 23p (cracker)

Items bought	Total cost	Change from 50p
1. star, bauble	35p	15p
2. snowman, cracker		
3. bird, bird, bird		
4. angel, cracker, holly		
5. santa, snowman, star		
6. bauble, bauble, angel		

Notes for teachers
Objective: Solve problems including money; finding totals and giving change.
An extension to this activity is to encourage pupils to make their own change sums by choosing any two or three items totalling 50p or less and calculating the change. If this is done, pupils can construct a table like the one given, to help them to present their work clearly.

worksheet 34

Change from £5

Name: Date:

Work out the change from £5.00 for the following items:

A chocolate Santa for £1.50.
Change from £5.00:

A Christmas tree for £4.50.
Change from £5.00:

A box of crackers for £3.50.
Change from £5.00:

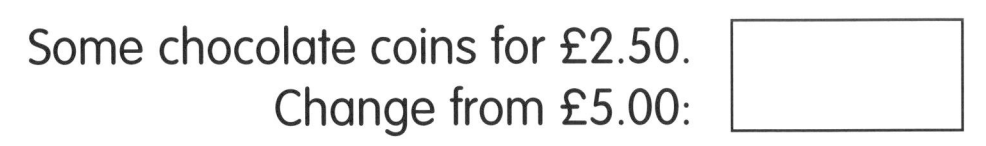

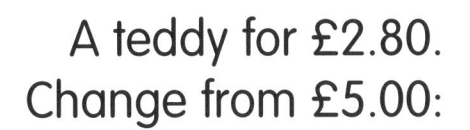

Some chocolate coins for £2.50.
Change from £5.00:

A teddy for £2.80.
Change from £5.00:

Notes for teachers
Objective: Solve problems including money; finding totals and giving change.
Many children make a common mistake with this type of question, eg if asked to find the change from five pounds when spending one pound fifty pence. They are likely to give the answer 'four pounds fifty pence'. To avoid this, encourage them to use a number line from £0 to £5, marked every fifty pence, then to count on from £1.50 to £2, then from £2 to £5.

Worksheet 35: Bells in squares

Name:　　　　　　　　　　　　　　　　　　　　Date:

Draw a bell on square number 1.
Count on two and draw another bell.
Keep counting on in twos. Colour each bell yellow.

1	2	3	4	5
6	7	8	9	10
11	12	13	14	15
16	17	18	19	20
21	22	23	24	25

Answer the questions.

1 + 2 = ☐　　　13 + 2 = ☐　　　5 + 2 = ☐

17 + 2 = ☐　　　9 + 2 = ☐　　　23 + 2 = ☐

Notes for teachers
Objective: Describe and extend number sequences
Encourage the children to observe the pattern that the bells make. They may notice that all the bell squares are odd numbers.

Worksheet 36: Two each

Name: Date:

1 child has 2 presents. $1 \times 2 = 2$

2 children have 2 presents each. $2 \times 2 =$ ☐

3 children have 2 presents each. $3 \times 2 =$ ☐

4 children have 2 presents each. $4 \times 2 =$ ☐

5 children have 2 presents each. $5 \times 2 =$ ☐

6 children have 2 presents each. $6 \times 2 =$ ☐

7 children have 2 presents each. $7 \times 2 =$ ☐

8 children have 2 presents each. $8 \times 2 =$ ☐

9 children have 2 presents each. $9 \times 2 =$ ☐

10 children have 2 presents each. $10 \times 2 =$ ☐

Write out your two times table on the back of this sheet. Can you say it without looking?

Notes for teachers
Objective: Know multiplication facts for the 2 times table
Children can build up their two times table by counting the presents. As an extension, higher ability pupils could try to work out how many presents there are altogether on the page: ie 2 + 4 + 6 + 8 , etc. (110 in total).

Andrew Brodie: Christmas Maths 5–7 © A & C Black Publishers Ltd. 2006

Worksheet 37

Light up the house

Name:

Date:

Colour red the lights that belong to the two times table.
Colour the other lights a different colour.

Two times table

Notes for teachers
Objective: Know multiplication facts for the 2 times table
This is a good consolidation and assessment task. Encourage the pupils to say their two times table as they work. They may notice that all the answers are even numbers.

Worksheet 38: Light up the sleigh

Name:

Date:

Colour blue the lights that belong to the ten times table.
Colour the other lights a different colour.

Lights on the sleigh: 17, 40, 15, 23, 90, 6, 36, 10, 60, 100, 9, 31, 42, 72, 80, 81, 30, 11, 13, 22, 24, 71, 20, 14, 50, 7, 70, 12

Ten times table

Notes for teachers
Objective: Know multiplication facts for the 10 times table
This is a good consolidation and assessment task. Encourage the pupils to say their ten times table as they work. They may notice that all the answers have a zero as the units digit.

Worksheet 39: Light up the tree

Name:
Date:

Colour red the lights that belong to the five times table. Colour the other lights a different colour.

Numbers on the tree: 36, 45, 60, 11, 5, 57, 12, 9, 18, 14, 40, 44, 10, 94, 35, 72, 21, 30, 50, 20, 16, 56, 28, 15, 96, 64, 25, 16, 32

Five times table

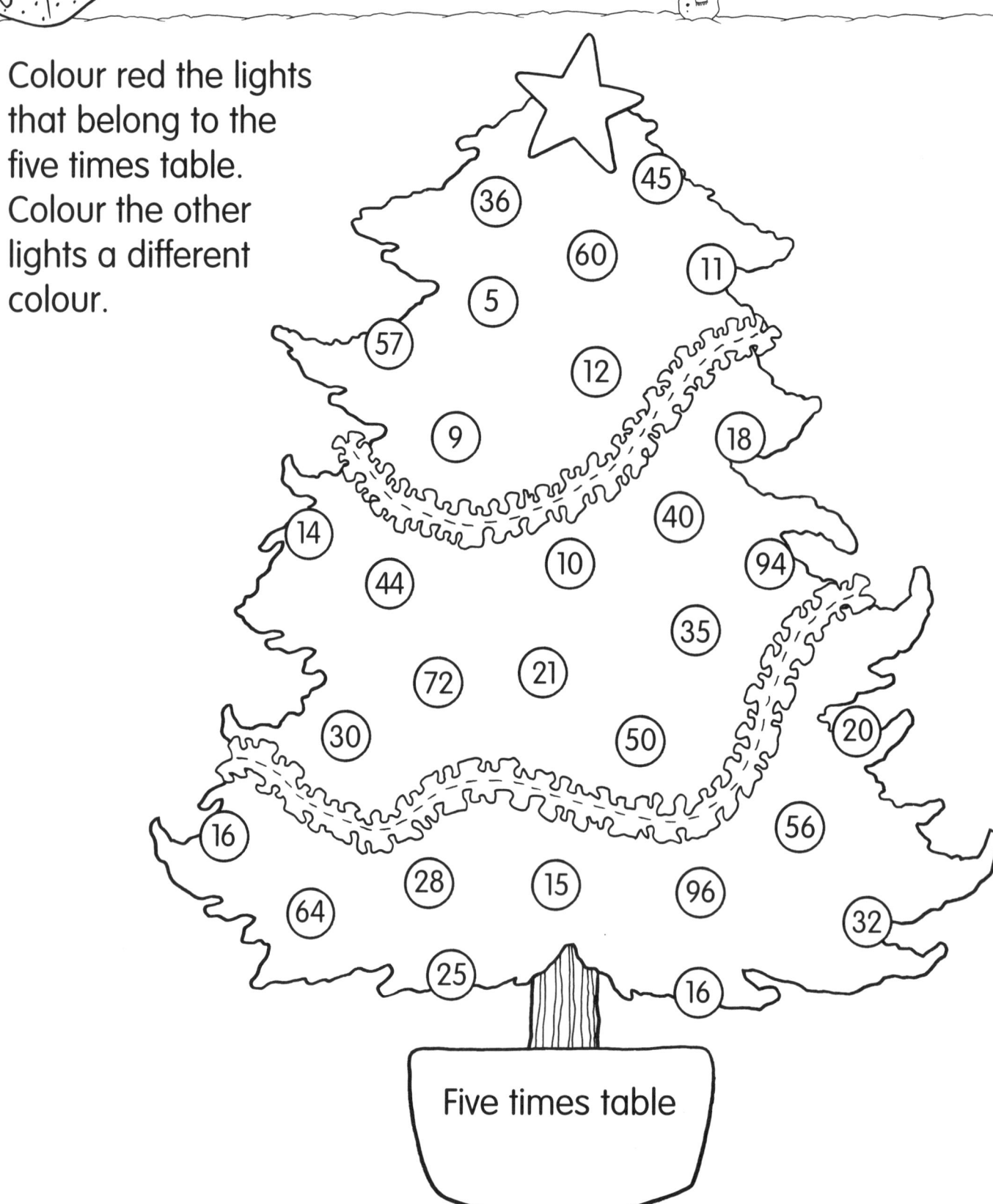

Notes for teachers
Objective: Begin to know multiplication facts for the 5 times table
This is a good consolidation and assessment task. Encourage the pupils to say their five times table as they work. They may notice that all the answers have either a zero or a five as the units digit.

Worksheet 40

Christmas timetable

Name: Date:

Draw lines to match each clock to the correct picture.
Then colour the pictures.

At half past 4 Father Christmas and his helpers began to load the sleigh.

At 9 o'clock the reindeer ate some hay before starting on their journey.

At 10 o'clock the sleigh was flying high up in the sky.

At half past seven on Christmas morning Santa climbed into bed after a busy night delivering presents.

Now you may colour the pictures.

Notes for teachers
Objective: Read the time to the nearest hour and half hour
Ensure the children understand that the clocks are not in the same order as the pictures.

Andrew Brodie: Christmas Maths 5–7 © A & C Black Publishers Ltd. 2006

Worksheet 41

Measuring up

Name: Date:

Use a ruler to measure the dotted lines to the nearest whole centimetre. When you have measured the lines you may decorate the tree.

cm

cm

cm

cm

cm

cm

cm

cm

cm

cm

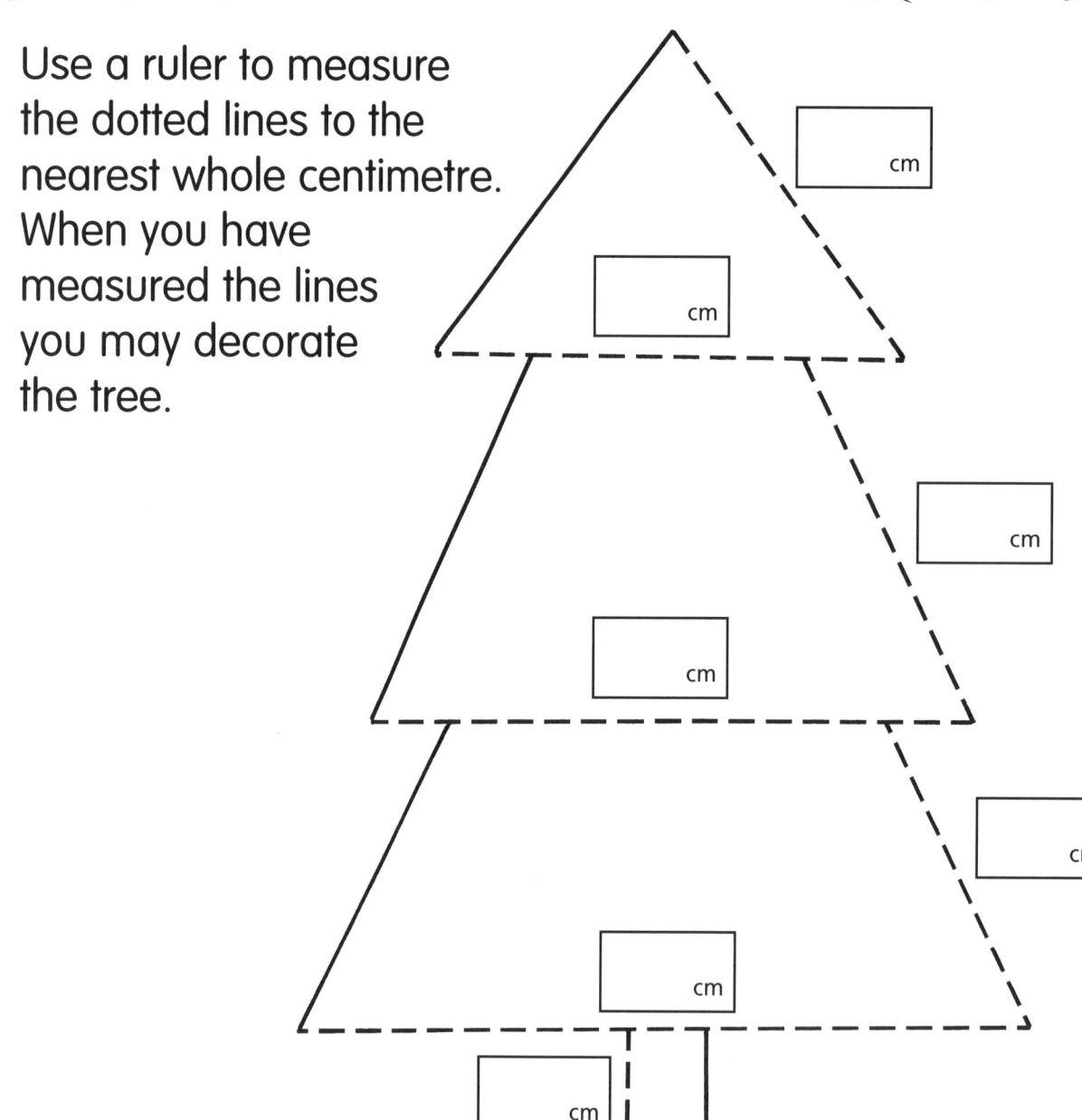

Notes for teachers
Objective: Measure lines to the nearest centimetre
Make sure that the children start measuring from the zero line on the ruler. They may need help in recognising 'the nearest centimetre'. An extension to this activity would be to ask pupils to draw some rectangular gifts near the base of the tree and to specify how long each gift should be.

44   Andrew Brodie: Christmas Maths 5–7 © A & C Black Publishers Ltd. 2006

Worksheet 42

Santa's sleigh

Name: Date:

Look at the picture of Santa in his sleigh.
Measure the dotted lines.
Colour the picture.

[ ] cm

[ ] cm

[ ] cm

[ ] cm

[ ] cm

Notes for teachers
Objective: Measure lines to the nearest centimetre
An extension to this activity would be to ask pupils to measure other parts of the picture. These of course might not be exact centimetre lengths, giving you the opportunity to talk about expressing their measurement as nearly X centimetres or just over X centimetres.

Andrew Brodie: Christmas Maths 5–7 © A & C Black Publishers Ltd. 2006

Worksheet 43 — All year round

Name: Date:

Copy the names of the months.

- January   ------------------------------
- February   ------------------------------
- March   ------------------------------
- April   ------------------------------
- May   ------------------------------
- June   ------------------------------
- July   ------------------------------
- August   ------------------------------
- September   ------------------------------
- October   ------------------------------
- November   ------------------------------
- December   ------------------------------

Christmas is in December.
In which month is your birthday? ------------------------------

Notes for teachers
Objective: Know in order the months of the year
This is both a spelling and a 'time' activity. Encourage the children to learn the order of the months. You could initiate a class discussion about events that happen each month, eg, 'We go to the beach in July'.

Christmas countdown

worksheet 44

Name: Date:

1	2	3	4	5	6	7
8	9	10	11	12	13	14
15	16	17	18	19	20	21
22	23	24 Christmas Eve	25	26 Boxing Day	27	28
29	30	31				

Christmas Day is on 25th December.

There are thirty-one days in December.
Colour the even numbers green.
Colour the odd numbers red.

Is Christmas Day on an even date or an odd date?

Notes for teachers
Objective: Know significant times in the year
This activity is about odd and even numbers as well as gaining understanding about a significant time in the year. You could discuss that December is the last month of the year and that therefore 31st December is New Year's Eve. Many children will not have appreciated that 'eve' signifies the day before an event.

Andrew Brodie: Christmas Maths 5–7 © A & C Black Publishers Ltd. 2006

Christmas Su Doku

Name: **Date:**

Every box ⊞ must have 🎄 ❄ 🎁 ☃

Every row ▭▭▭▭ must have 🎄 ❄ 🎁 ☃

Every column ▯ must have 🎄 ❄ 🎁 ☃

Can you fill all the squares?

Notes for teachers
Objective: Solve mathematical puzzles
Encourage the children to colour each of the symbols differently so that it will be easier for them to fill the gaps.